Be Angry and Sin Not

Edited by Myra Chave-Jones

**Dr. Ruth Fowke, Rev. Dick Keyes
Rev. John Stott**

Scripture Union
130, City Road, London EC1V 2NJ

© 1983 Care and Counsel
146 Queen Victoria Street, London EC4

First published 1983
Reprinted 1984
ISBN 0 86201 162 0

Printed in Great Britain by
Scripture Union
130 City Road, London EC1V 2NJ

Introduction

Everyone knows about anger. It is surprising that so little is said or written about it in the Christian world. There seems to be a general impression that the biblical teaching amounts to 'Do not be angry'.

The Council of Management of *Care and Counsel* decided to convene a half day conference to consider the subject of the Christian management of anger. It was held on Saturday 16 October 1976, at St. Helen's Church, Bishopsgate, London. The speakers were Dr. Ruth Fowke (consultant psychiatrist) and the Rev. Dick Keyes (former minister of the l'Abri Church, Ealing). The Chairman, the Rev. John Stott, added a summary.

There was some discussion in small groups but the subject is so great and experience so varied that it was impossible to deal with the topic adequately in the time allowed. The Council of Management decided, therefore, to produce this monograph which would expand some of the issues raised. The object is to provoke further thought, not to provide all the answers. The material is drawn from the contributions of the speakers and the Chairman, and is edited and expanded by Myra Chave-Jones.

The Anger Of God

This topic sounds more appropriate for thundering Puritans or stern Victorians. It is thought by some to be a fairly barbarous subject for the sophisticated twentieth century. Certainly it would seem as though many modern Christians have lost the sense of the holiness of God (and consequently of the wrath of God) as displayed in parts of the Old and New Testaments.

Our embarrassment in contemplating God's anger is connected with our misunderstanding of it. Sometimes God's anger is envisaged as an overpowering, disproportionate fury which threatens to devour our impotent efforts, or else as some unfortunate lapse in a mainly benevolent personality. Both these views are out of line with scripture and are highly subjective.

The Father

We need to understand *the nature of God's anger* and 'disabuse ourselves of the idea that it is ever capricious, self-indulgent, irritable, or morally ignoble' (J.I. Packer, *Knowing God*; Hodder and Stoughton). It is true that God's anger cannot be taken lightly, as implied in the words of Nahum 1:6,

> '. . . Who can stand before his indignation?
> Who can endure the heat of his anger?
> His wrath is poured out like fire
> And the rocks are broken asunder by him.'

Nevertheless, Moses was able to tolerate the extreme heat of God's anger and to have a dialogue with him for forty days and nights (Deut. 9:13–29). That must have been one of the most illuminating experiences of his life. The quality of God's anger was indeed fearful but it was 'safe'. (Most people's experience is that human anger is usually unreasonable, unpredictable and uncontrolled and therefore the wisest course of action is to disappear rapidly.)

A study of God's anger, whenever it is revealed and against whoever it is directed, always leads to the same conclusion. Here are some examples:

Aaron's flagrant flaunting of God's known purposes (though he was in a position of leadership) made God 'so angry that he was ready to destroy him' (Deut. 9:20).

4

Moses repeated the sad lament three times: 'the Lord was angry with me on your account and swore that I should not enter into the good land . . .' – because he had misrepresented God to the people at the waters of Meribah (Deut. 1:37; 3:26; 4:21).

Achan's personal greed made him disregard the clear instructions of the God whose intention was to present himself as holy, and his people as different from the nations round about: '. . . but the people broke faith, for Achan took some of the devoted things, and the anger of the Lord burned against the people' (Josh. 7:1).

Solomon's self-indulgent decadence was more important to him than the twice repeated personal command of the God of Israel, with the consequence that '. . . the Lord was very angry with Solomon because his heart had turned away' (1 Kings 11:9).

Israel's ingratitude, grumbling, faithlessness, cowardice and persistent failure to keep their own word are all too familiar; '. . . therefore the Lord was very angry with Israel and removed them out of his sight . . .' (2 Kings 17:18).

It is all summed up in the words of Ezra 8:22: 'the power of his wrath is against all that forsake him' – in whatever way they turn to other guidelines for life. God's anger is about his eternal justice, his own righteousness and his love which is beyond the comprehension of a human mind. God's anger does not simply reveal his attitude, it is also the necessary consequence of an inevitable process of cause and effect in a moral universe. But that does not mean a mechanical and relentless process; the same men who speak of God's anger speak in detail about God's mercy, his sorrow and his compassion:

> '. . . The Lord is merciful and gracious
> Slow to anger and abounding in steadfast love'
>
> (Ps. 103:8).

The Son

In Jesus Christ we see the nature of God, because Jesus said of himself, 'I and the Father are one'.

Surprisingly, there is very little material about Jesus's anger. The only explicit reference is in Mark 3:5: 'he looked around at them with anger, grieved at their hardness of heart. . .'

In this incident, however, there is ample evidence that Jesus *felt* intense anger against the silent, merciless, legalistic attitude of the men standing around and that he *displayed* his anger openly against those who aroused it.

Another word, implying anger of a different intensity, is used of the disciples when they discovered that James and John were conspiring to obtain seats One and Two in the Kingdom (Mark 10:41). It is also used of the reaction of the chief priests and scribes after Jesus had cleansed the Temple: they were 'indignant' (Matt. 21:15).

That same word is used to describe Jesus' attitude when his disciples tried, in their underestimation of him, to protect him from the demands of parents and children. He did not merely *feel* indignant, he *said* and *did* something about it (Mark 10:13–16).

A third specific word indicating that Jesus felt and expressed anger is found in Mark 1:43, Matthew 9:30 and John 11:33, 38; the Greek word means 'to snort with anger, as of horses'. The text implies that Jesus approached the grave of Lazarus in a state, not only of intense grief, but also of intense anger and rage. It was as though the distress of Martha and Mary brought home to his consciousness again the evil of death, its unnaturalness and 'violent tyranny'; the general misery of the whole human race – and behind it 'him who has the power of death'. The raising of Lazarus, therefore, became a decisive instance and open symbol of Jesus' conquest of death and hell.

A fourth word relating to Jesus' anger occurs many times in the accounts of his daily interaction with people; it is translated variously as *rebuked, charged, strictly charged, commanded, ordered*. The rebuke to Peter, 'Get behind me, Satan!' (Mark 8:33) was not a mild admonition; it was a sharp comparison intended to puncture Peter's complacency.

There is also a list of public denunciations – *fox, swine, whited sepulchres, ravening wolves, sons of vipers, children of your father the Devil* – which can hardly be taken as terms of endearment!

All these are expressions of Jesus' anger against various forces opposing God. He was deeply incensed by anything which was an indication of the works of the Devil, whose works he had come to destroy. But we never have the impression that he was irascible or petty, or that he was angry with people because he did not get on well with them.

Clearly God, as seen in Jesus Christ, is sometimes described as being very angry indeed and so we can establish the point that, as we are made in the image of God, anger can be a good and right part of human experience. This runs counter to the common idea among some Christians that anger is always a reprehensible trait.

The Anger Of Man

At once we feel uncomfortable. Anger is unpleasant; it produces acute physical sensations, heavy atmospheres, and a disturbance of equilibrium. It is often felt to be so overwhelmingly destructive that we fear it in ourselves and feel threatened when we see it in others.

Our instinctive reaction is to avoid it and sometimes, in so doing, we forget the scriptural model. We over-emphasise the 'love, joy, peace' aspect of Christian behaviour because that seems more acceptable, and forget the fact that we are told to 'be angry'.

Anger is energy

The study of positive anger and the constructive use of it is a much neglected subject. It is because we so often use anger wrongly that we suppose it to be wrong in itself. The impulse to anger is, in fact, morally neutral, like hunger or ambition. Dr. Theodore Isaac Rubin, former president of the American Institute of Pyscho-analysis, says:

> 'Getting angry is neither right nor wrong. People who seek justification are attempting to rationalise or excuse their anger because they don't quite accept it. Getting angry, like getting hungry, is a human phenomenon, and neither needs an excuse for being. If someone is hungry, he is hungry . . . The same is true for anger. If he is angry, he is angry regardless of any right or wrong issues involved. There is simply no right or wrong or moral evaluation here.
>
> (Dr. Theodore Rubin, The Angry Book
McMillan-Collier, New York 1969.)

Anger takes on a moral dimension when it is put into use. We can discover the potential that lies in anger once we can get away from its negative aspects. In the *General Confession* we ask for forgiveness of our sins of omission and commission: the sins of omission come first and among them should be the times when we have not been angry when we ought to have been.

Anger is energy. We should be angry about things that are wrong around us and then use the energy to get the wrong put right. Where should we be today if Shaftesbury and Wilberforce had not been angry at the conditions they found a century or so ago and which were accepted by their contemporaries?

We are also too complacent about our Adversary. We either blame him for everything (especially our own short-comings) or we effectively discount his activity. We should not just be against him in theory, in a rather passive and negative way, but be positively, actively angry about the things he does in our world, to us and to our friends.

How we can be angry with the originator of sin yet not with the sinner does remain a problem. Handling righteous anger is difficult: handling unrighteous anger is even more difficult. Nevertheless, both forms of anger exist and they must be handled and not hidden away.

The results of non-expression of anger

What happens when we do not express our anger, either because we do not recognise it or, if we do recognise it, if we stifle it very quickly? We can consider the effects under two headings.

Physiological: The pulse rate goes up, blood pressure rises, breathing gets faster, and blood is diverted to the brain and limbs from the stomach (so if you eat when you are angry you may get indigestion). The purpose of this mechanism is to prepare the whole body for fight or flight. The brain releases chemicals which react on the glands through the body. The net result is an increase in adrenalin and other substances which, once in circulation, further stimulate the brain. So we get a chain reaction, and the response to anger is inevitably prolonged.

In anger there is a complex series of physiological changes of mind and body which are very much interrelated. We cannot affect one without the other. If the response to anger is prolonged, that is to say, has no proper outlet leading to the relaxation of the body and its return to a normal resting state, then the body's total response to anger is one factor which contributes to such problems as peptic ulcers, hypertension, asthma, eczema, tension headaches and a host of other ills. (*Please note* that not all sufferers from these illnesses are necessarily angry people, and not all angry people suffer from one of these illnesses. Genetic, and a number of other factors, are also involved.)

Psychological: Various theories about the origins of anger have been propounded down the years. Originally it was said that the emotion of anger is due solely to physiological changes which derive from external stimuli.

Later, Freud and subsequent psycho-analysts stated that tensions and conflicts which are too painful and dangerous to tolerate consciously lie buried, deep in the unconscious mind. Life begins in a state of blissful dependence, but the experience of birth and subsequent weaning, toilet training, and the demand to conform to numerous other social conventions, begin a long process of frustrations. Depending on the quality of the relationship between the adult and child, these experiences can contribute positively to the production of a mature and reasonably equable personality.

On the other hand, a relationship which is full of conflict and mutual frustration can create anxieties and furies which are too threatening for an infant psyche and so these dread emotions are repressed and 'forgotten', only to re-appear later in sundry disguises. In the presence of appropriate stimuli these repressed emotions will make their presence felt in some way, though they may perhaps not be immediately identifiable. Disproportionate anger is one such manifestation.

Dr. Rubin describes this luridly in his section entitled *Twisting It: The Assorted Poisons*. He speaks of the conversion of healthy angry feelings and responses into a 'slush bank'. The perversions (mostly unconscious) include anxiety, depression, overeating and starvation, insomnia, obsessions, compulsions and phobias, bullying, sexual frigidity, boredom, etc.

Psychologists from the behaviourist school have formed their theories from observation of the behaviour of animals, and maintain that anger/aggression is a reflex action to any stimulus which threatens or frustrates; for instance, a cat's fur stands on end in the presence of an enemy. Thus, to defend oneself in the face of danger and on occasions to react angrily, is a self-protective instinct. Moral judgements on such behaviour are inappropriate.

Remembering that anger is energy, it does not surprise us that lack of anger leads to apathy. Most of us know the withdrawn person without sparkle or spirit, who tends to underachieve at work, socially or in some other sphere; and it is only a very short step from apathy to depression.

For practical purposes we can distinguish five types of depression:
1) A biochemical condition which has little or nothing to do with anger or emotion.
2) A reaction to loss of some sort.
3) Social dis-ease.

Both 2) and 3) can be connected with angry feelings which have not been expressed and are turned in on themselves.
4) A normal state, the natural consequence of prolonged and intense activity, forcing the person to slow down and recuperate, if only he will heed nature's warning.
5) A spiritual malady.

The value of anger

Aggression, a word we hear a lot about today, is the motor counterpart of anger. Some of our everyday sayings illustrate how much we need aggression for problem solving and intellectual maturity. We 'attack a situation', 'get our teeth into a problem', 'sharpen our wits', 'strive to overcome', and so on.

We need anger and aggression and are the poorer if we disown this part of our make-up. To be human is to be angry at times. Hopefully those times are appropriate and not inappropriate, but a person who is never angry is not fully a person.

The converse is not necessarily true (that to be angry is to be human) because excess anger is very dehumanising.

The most difficult patients whom a psychiatrist has to try to help are those who can never show anger or any other emotion – they are totally apathetic and withdrawn. The long-stay wards in any psychiatric hospital contain far more of these sort of people than the angry dangerous people who occasionally make news.

We speak of 'an angry rash' which is another indication of how closely the mind, body and spirit are connected in response to a situation – not one part reacting independently of the others, but the total person responding as a whole unit.

Dr. Rubin says 'I believe that you feel either all your feelings or eventually none at all. You cannot select which feelings you will feel and which you won't . . . Negate anger and you must also negate love . . . Anger and love and the feeling of both do not operate in separate compartments or in separate people. We cannot reject one and hope to experience the other.' (One reviewer of this book writes: 'If Dr. Rubin's comments are correct, the screamers among us are doing all right. But watch out for those cold and quiet cats!') Clearly, therefore, anger is a purposeful attribute which, in its proper place, is a necessary and healthy part of human nature.

The significance of anger

1. It draws attention to a blockage in communication.

In an angry exchange between two people there are always responsive messages. The angry wife is not mollified by a soothing husband who says literally or metaphorically 'There, there, dear, you'll soon feel better'. He may thereby be saying in effect 'I think you are a baby' or 'Don't bother me now' or 'I don't intend to meet your need' or 'Don't take any notice: she's just being herself' – and certainly conveys the impression that he does not understand or does not want to make the effort to do so. He need not be surprised if the anger goes smouldering or flaming on!

Anger (in our relationships) is often a symptom of a machine which needs some oil, and it is a good thing to pay attention to the squeaks before the machine seizes up. Anger is often a message of desperation when all other means seem to have failed. Often an outburst about some trivial incident is simply saying, 'You are not listening to the messages I am trying to give you'. But we can only listen if we are sufficiently free in ourselves from the fear and threat which anger engenders.

2. It can indicate love.

The lack of appropriate anger between parent and outrageous adolescent can too often be interpreted as lack of love and concern, not as extended tolerance. Many a young person is heard to lament: 'If only my parents had cared', meaning that anger is preferable to indifference; and anger which is known to be born of love is a powerful influence.

3. It can indicate appreciation of the value of a person who is set on pursuing some self-destructive objective.

The angry protest is sometimes the only way in which the person who undervalues himself can be made to reconsider what he is doing.

4. It can allow the release of frustrations,

as in the 'teddy bear' syndrome: husbands and wives (and indeed any friends) often play this role for each other. A child in trouble will go upstairs and pulverise his teddy until he turns to it for a cuddle and a sleep. It is important for teddy to be able to understand the messages here – for if he starts fighting back there could be worse trouble! The messages of anger can be very complex and involve hurt, fear, shame, love, and discovery, amongst other things.

The connection between anger and sex is significant. The end result of these intimate exchanges, if handled constructively, can be a great increase in communication, in self-understanding, growth, and in understanding between partners. Thus there can be some important outcomes of anger: (a) real strides towards maturity, (b) increased ability to tolerate the pain which anger produces and therefore, (c) a more realistic ability in handling it.

5. It can indicate an inner, personal conflict.

Most people have at times been amazed by the irritational intensity of their angry feelings about some general subject which is not immediately related to them personally – be it immigration, women drivers, or Americans. This is sometimes an indication of an inner personal conflict which threatens to undermine their equilibrium. If it were recognised, identified, and dealt with, greater inner peace could be achieved.

6. It can indicate a lack of maturity.

There is the unnecessarily angry over-reaction of one person to a situation which leaves the other people feeling puzzled and helpless. For instance, in a staff team the newest colleague may become defensively angry. This anger is not appropriate to the actual situation but could be to do with some unfinished business of childhood rivalry with older brothers and sisters which is being transposed into the adult situation at work.

The management of anger

The trouble is that anger so often gets out of control and then we fear the very thing we need in life. Indeed the reasons for our anger are often closely related to fear. The very words *anger* and *anxiety* are related in origin. Anger and fear between them are either responsible for, or a major factor in, every emotional turmoil that besets us.

But both are consistently mishandled by earnest well-meaning Christians. It is useless to quote verses at an angry or fearful person telling him not to be; that only increases his sense of failure, rejection, condemnation and personal despair. We cannot help another person with his anger and fear if we have not acccepted these two emotions in ourselves. Acceptance is the beginning of proper control and utilisation.

Helen was fairly newly pregnant. She felt distinctly fragile. She had had a very busy day at her work, had rushed home to go to the launderette and give the house a quick clean and, hot and tired, was busy cooking the evening meal. At 9 p.m. her young husband breezed in from his busy day, full of life and chat, and running his finger across the top of the cooker remarked 'Mmm – some time since you gave this a good clean! And, by the way, isn't it time you wrote to my mother?' Seconds later he was standing amazed, with leeks, ham, sauce, etc. dripping from his face.

How should this Christian couple have handled this situation? Psalm 4:4, says, 'Be angry but sin not: commune with your own hearts on your beds and be silent'. Should Helen have gone quietly upstairs and half an hour later returned, all sweetness and light, to continue her work? Yes, possibly, but things don't usually happen like that on the spur of the moment. In the heat of the instant, beds and silence seem too far away. The wisdom of 'commune with your hearts on your beds and be silent' needs to be explained more clearly.

Primarily, it means that we must try to understand the messages that we are getting from other people and from our own selves. We need to ask ourselves questions like: 'Have I provoked this by my own sheer thoughtlessness, preoccupation, self-centredness? What is the other person trying to tell me? Is there some other problem quite unrelated to the one which provoked the row? Am I prepared to be in the wrong? What lies underneath these attitudes? Am I prepared to modify my position?' Sometimes the immediate answer to the last question is 'No', and so we go on communing – sometimes for days – until we can 'accept the humbler part and o'er our *own* shortcomings weep with loathing'.

It is vital to identify the proper cause, to listen to what our emotions are saying to us, to befriend them rather than distrust them, and then to ask the Holy Spirit to do something about it or to show us what we can do.

The main value of a row is that we can be made more self-aware. There are some unattractive aspects of ourselves of which we are unaware until someone collides with them and is prepared to challenge and wrestle with them. One partner, for instance, may need to have his domineering traits challenged in order that the other partner can begin to stop taking the line of 'peace at any price'. This line results too often in smouldering rage, depression or some psychosomatic symptom, all of which are too high a price to pay for spurious peace.

The all important proviso is '. . . but do not sin: let not the sun go down upon your wrath'. Anger is not static: it either grows or abates but it does not stand still. It is therefore important to deal with the *external* effects of anger quickly and to apologise or take whatever action is appropriate to restore communication.

We have a tremendous tendency to nurse grievances and this most certainly leads to sin. Anger, like a baby, grows stronger when it is nursed. It is not necessarily sin of itself but if not acknowledged and dealt with can result in sinful behaviour, which then provokes a sinful response which sparks off another sinful retort . . .

However, the *deep causes* of anger may need much longer than the arrival of sunset for their understanding and healing. It is a mistake to think that an absence of open warfare implies peace and growth. It is comparatively easy to sweep the whole soreness under the carpet with vague words about the love and forgiveness of God without working out *fully* what is actually wrong. If the hard and often painful work of confrontation is bypassed (be it confrontation of myself by myself, or with another person) this anger situation will undoubtedly recur with the same results. The pain of confrontation involves honesty and humility and courage.

It is sometimes hard to deal with anger if one has been brought up on the reasoning:

> 'I need to be loved: people love me when I am nice: anger is not nice: therefore I must not be angry and anger is bad.'

Trustful relationships are essential for personal growth. Within such relationships it is possible to experience unconditional love in spite of angry feelings and unpleasantness.

Our anger has been affected by the fall (as have our love, pity, joy, etc.) and so is often directed against the wrong things, and in ways which are unconstructive: this is what can make it 'wrong'. Aristotle describes a meek person as 'angry on the right occasion and with the right people and at the right moment and for the right length of time'. William Barclay adds, 'Blessed is the man who is always angry at the right time and never angry at the wrong time' (*Gospel of Matthew* Vol. 1; St. Andrew's Press).

Granted that in mixed-up creatures like us (who are what we are because of creation, the fall and redemption) probably none of our anger is wholly righteous or unrighteous: all reactions are mixed with elements of each. Nevertheless we must learn to distinguish between the 'righteous' and 'unrighteous' motives of anger in order to know how to cope with it.

When we are protesting hotly about some wrong done to us, can we be sure that it is all *pure* anger against the injustice of the situation?

'Righteous' anger is aroused by outrages directed against God, others or ourselves. It is important to know when, how and whether to express it. It is not wrong to protest against personal injustice. Jesus did this by his deafening silence at his own trial.

In some cases it is not possible to confront someone with the anger which is being aroused: parents, for example, who are already dead but are experienced as having left a trail of blood; or sick and dependent relatives, whose very sickness and dependency produces pain and anger with the illness.

It is helpful to share this in total honesty with the Lord, who has in his own body absorbed murderous anger and not been finally destroyed by it, instead of letting guilt mount up with the anger. But even so, there are times when the presence of a third person who knows how to help in this sort of situation is important.

Summary

RIGHTEOUS ANGER
Cultivate it
Social injustice is a proper object of Christian anger. Not to be angry about that is a sin of omission. The Devil and all his works should provoke us to anger. When Paul wandered around Athens and saw that the city was full of false gods he was 'provoked' in spirit. Jesus Christ was grieved when he saw things that were incompatible with the good purposes of God. He could neither remain unmoved, nor condone them.

So let us cultivate more righteous anger. Think of the results of William Booth's investigation into the state of England in the nineteenth century; or Shaftesbury's horror about labour conditions in the factories and the mines; or Barnardo's indignation about the fate of homeless children. We should reflect on the evils that we can see and know about today, and *why* they are displeasing to God, until the fires of indignation burn. Is it because there is not enough righteous anger that so much unrighteousness abounds?

Have the courage to express it
We are often too afraid to be angry. We dare not express it lest we lose either our reputation for being able to keep our equilibrium, or the friendship of the people who make us angry. Jesus did not commend himself to the traders whose tables he overturned!

Make sure it leads to action
All emotions are dangerous if they do not have a constructive outlet. It is no good 'feeling compassion' for the hungry if we do not write a cheque or *do* something.

Neither is it any good 'feeling angry' if we do not take corrective action. Anger has constructive (as opposed to destructive) potential. Jesus was indignant about disease so he healed it, and about death so he raised Lazarus.

There is also a place for rebuking individuals:

> 'Anger is indeed necessary sometimes, but only in those whose responsibility it is, and only if it does not go beyond the punishment of sin and evil. Thus when you see another man sinning, and you warn and urge him to stop it, such anger is Christian and brotherly, yes, even fatherly ... In other words, it is an anger of love; one that wishes no-one any evil; one that is friendly to the person, but hostile to the sin ... But it is not right to use this as a screen for hiding and decorating the malice and envy of our hearts against our neighbour ...'
>
> (Martin Luther, *Sermon on the Mount.* Pelikan's Translation, Concordia Publications.)

UNRIGHTEOUS ANGER

Jesus reminded his hearers of the seriousness of anger 'without cause' (Matt. 5:21). James says that 'the anger of man does not work the righteousness of God' (Jas. 1:20).

There are some steps we can take to help ourselves in looking at our anger:

Admit it

We must recognise it in order to deal with and defuse it. We must resist trying to make excuses for ourselves or rationalising our reactions.

Reflect on it and try to understand it (Ps. 4:4)

We need to talk to ourselves about it. What has provoked this outburst? What has been upset? My own self-esteem? My personal preferences? Has someone pushed me further than I am willing to go? Do I need to think about this and assess my present tolerance level so that next time in a similar situation I can begin to react differently? Where are my resources coming from to meet this sort of thing. What about *God* as my vindicator? Whatever became of my sense of humour?

Thus we can grow in self-knowledge, in faith and in Christlikeness.

Pray for those who have done us injustice

Since anger is energy, it is better to be positive and to convert it into prayer rather than anxiety, depression, over-eating, starvation.

Share it with the person concerned

Face it together, apologise, forgive and grow. There is no fellowship so deep as that of people who have exposed themselves, been hurt, penitent and forgiven.

Seek the help of a third person if necessary

In conclusion, the whole matter is encompassed in the words of Ephesians 4:26, 27 (NIV):

> **In your anger do not sin. Do not let the sun go down while you are still angry, and do not give the devil a foothold.**